The Declaration of Independence

KAREN PRICE HOSSELL

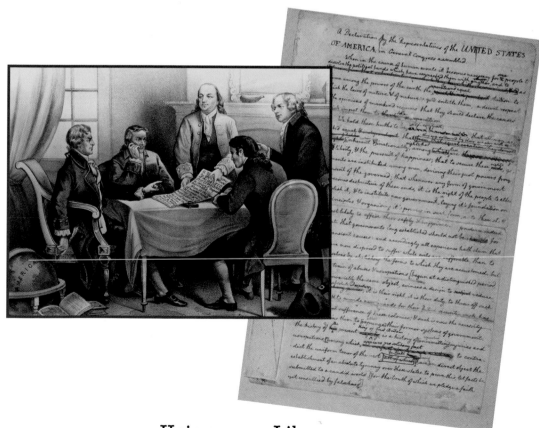

Heinemann Library
Chicago, Illinois

© 2004 Heinemann Library,
a division of Reed Elsevier Inc.
Chicago, Illinois

Customer Service 888-454-2279
Visit our website at www.heinemannlibrary.com

Designed by Herman Adler Design
Photo research by Bill Broyles
Printed and bound in the United States by Lake Book Manufacturing, Inc.

08 07 06 05 04
10 9 8 7 6 5 4 3 2

Library of Congress Cataloging-in-Publication Data
Price Hossell, Karen, 1957-
   The Declaration of Independence / Karen Price Hossell.
      v. cm. -- (Historical documents)
Includes bibliographical references (p.) and index.
Contents: Recording important events -- Storing valuable documents -- What is the Declaration of Independence? -- Taxing the colonies -- Boycotts and protests -- The colonies band together -- Drafting the document -- Jefferson writes the Declaration -- Congress revises the Declaration -- Independence -- Americans hear the news -- The Introduction -- The Preamble -- The List of Grievances -- The Denunciation of the British People -- The Conclusion -- Engrossing the Declaration -- Travels of the Declaration -- The Declaration on display -- Working with the Declaration.
   ISBN 1-4034-0802-5 (lib. bdg.) -- ISBN 1-4034-3431-X (pbk.)
   1. United States. Declaration of Independence--Juvenile literature.
   2. United States--Politics and government--1775-1783--Juvenile literature. [1. United States. Declaration of Independence. 2. United
States--Politics and government--1775-1783.] I. Title. II. Historical documents (Heinemann Library (Firm))
   E221.P75 2003
   973.3'13--dc21

                    2003008193

Acknowledgments
The author and publisher are grateful to the following for permission to reproduce copyright material:

Cover photographs by (document) National Archives and Records Administration; (clockwise from top) Hector Emanuel/Heinemann Library, Bettmann/Corbis, The Corcoran Gallery of Art/Corbis/Bettmann/Corbis; (title bar) Corbis.

Title page, pp. 12b, 14, 18, 21, 23, 29, 32, 39 Library of Congress; pp. 4, 25, 28, 30, 34, 36, 42, 43, 44 National Archives and Records Administration; p. 5 Hector Emanuel/Heinemann Library; p. 6 Elliott Teel/DC Stock Photo; p. 7 Richard T. Nowitz/Corbis; pp. 8, 10, 12t, 13, 15, 16, 24, 35, 37, 40 Bettmann/Corbis; pp. 9, 31 Corbis; pp. 11, 17 The Granger Collection, NY; p. 20 Independence National Historical Park; p. 22 Hulton Archive/Getty Images; p. 27 Reuters NewMedia Inc./Corbis; p. 33 North Wind Picture Archives; p. 38 Angelica Lloyd Russell Gallery/Museum of Fine Arts, Boston; p. 41 AP Wide World Photo; p. 45 Evan Vucci/AP Wide World Photo.

Some words are shown in bold, **like this.** You can find out what they mean by looking in the glossary.

Contents

Recording Important Events

Throughout history, people have created documents so they will have records of important events. Documents may tell stories about how people lived, how significant discoveries were made, or what occurred during a war.

Documents that provide a historical record of something can be divided into two categories: **primary sources** and **secondary sources.**

Primary sources

When historians are studying what happened in the past, they prefer to use primary sources. This term refers to documents that provide a firsthand account of an event. Primary sources can include letters, diaries, newspaper articles, **pamphlets,** and other papers that were written by people who witnessed or were directly involved in a past event.

The original copy of the Declaration of Independence measures 24.25 by 29 inches (61.59 by 73.66 centimeters).

The Liberty Bell was made in Great Britain for the Pennsylvania State House in 1752. In 1753, it cracked the first time it was struck. When the British occupied Philadelphia in 1777, the Liberty Bell and other bells were removed and sent to various cities so the British would not use them to make cannon.

Primary sources can also include official papers that were carefully planned, often with much discussion and argument. The people involved in the planning and writing of these papers were careful to make sure the words in the documents expressed the exact thoughts and ideas they wanted them to. Official papers are usually a clear record of just what the authors intended to say.

Primary sources tell us, in the words of the people who lived during that time, what really happened. They are a kind of direct communication that has not been filtered through a lot of sources. Often, stories that are passed verbally from person to person change as they are told and retold. Facts may become muddled and confused, and information may be added or left out. Soon, the original story has completely changed.

This is why primary sources are so important. Over time, facts can be changed or twisted, accidentally or on purpose, so unwritten accounts of what happened in the past can be incorrect. To find out what really happened and why, historians need to rely on printed or handwritten primary sources.

Storing Valuable Documents

Because **primary sources** provide an important record of historical events, they are considered valuable. For that reason, the paper-and-ink documents are carefully handled and stored so that they will last a long time.

Documents that are considered valuable records of United States history are kept in several different places. The two institutions that hold most of these historical records are the Library of Congress and the National Archives and Records Administration, or NARA.

The Library of Congress

The Library of Congress is in Washington, D.C. It is a **federal** institution and also the largest library in the world. The library holds about 120 million items, including maps, books, and photographs. Its collection is available to members of **Congress** as well to as the rest of the American public.

The Library of Congress building in Washington, D.C., houses many important U.S. documents, and once stored the Declaration of Independence.

Since this picture was taken, a new display has been built at the NARA for the Declaration, the **Constitution,** and the **Bill of Rights.** Together, these documents are known as the **Charters** of Freedom.

The NARA

The NARA is another government agency. It manages all federal records. Besides paper documents, the NARA also holds films, photographs, posters, sound and video recordings, and other types of government records. The original documents in the NARA collection provide a history of the U.S. government. They also tell the story of American settlement, industry, and farming. In fact, documents and other **artifacts** detailing almost every aspect of American history can be found in the NARA collection.

Most of the documents at the NARA are stored in specially designed boxes. Since paper is made from plants, it contains acids. Over time, these acids can discolor paper, turning it so dark that the ink on it cannot be read. For this reason, NARA storage boxes are acid-free. The boxes are stored in fireproof, locked **stacks** at the NARA's 41 different facilities. The temperature and **humidity** in NARA storage areas are carefully controlled, because heat and humidity can **deteriorate** documents.

What Is the Declaration of Independence?

The Declaration of Independence is the formal announcement that the American **colonies** were breaking their ties with Great Britain. Because this document signaled the beginning of the United States, the Declaration of Independence is considered to be one of the most important documents in U.S. history.

In 1776, a committee of five members from the Continental **Congress** planned what ideas to put into the Declaration of Independence. The person who actually wrote it, though, was a young **statesman** from Virginia named Thomas Jefferson.

Know It

The Fourth of July was made a legal U.S. holiday in 1941, but it has been celebrated since 1776!

The Pennsylvania State House was the site of many important gatherings.

This painting was left unfinished after the artist's death. It depicts Congress voting on the Declaration of Independence.

The meeting of Congress in 1776 was only the second such meeting in U.S. history. Congress met for the first time in late 1775. That meeting was called the First Continental Congress. The 1776 meeting was called the Second Continental Congress. The meetings were organized because **colonists** were becoming concerned over the laws and taxes that Britain was forcing them to accept. After many months of trying to work out a peaceful compromise with Great Britain, Congress decided to declare independence.

A huge step

The Declaration of Independence was a huge step in U.S. history. By breaking all ties with Great Britain, Congress members had done something they could not undo. The **Revolutionary War** began in 1775. Many colonists still hoped that the colonies could find a way to work out a quick and peaceful end to the war. They wanted the colonies to remain British, but they also wanted a voice in Britain's **legislature**, called **Parliament**. Once the Declaration was written and approved, though, any thoughts of **reconciliation** ended. With the Declaration, the colonists were officially stating that they were willing to continue fighting for independence until one side or the other lost.

Taxing the Colonies

The American **colonies** were settled by people from Great Britain, many of whom came to America so they could practice their religion freely. In Britain, they were told how to worship. When certain religious groups—such as the **Puritans** and the **Quakers**—decided that they wanted to worship in a different way, they had to sail to the American colonies to do so. Other settlers came to the colonies not for religious reasons, but to find jobs or make their fortunes.

As the colonies grew, more towns and cities developed. People like **surveyors** needed to draw the boundaries between the different areas of land.

Colonial government

The colonies were ruled by the king of Great Britain, George III, and by Britain's lawmaking body, called **Parliament.** Those who lived in the colonies were considered to be British **subjects.**

Each colony had its own form of government and its own group of lawmakers called a **legislature.** Britain, however, sent governors to the colonies to act as overseers. The colonies could make their own laws, but they still had to follow any laws that Parliament passed. In the early years of settlement, this arrangement usually worked out well.

War debts

In the middle of the eighteenth century, however, events occurred that changed how many **colonists** viewed their British rulers. From 1754 to 1763, Britain, with the help of many American colonists, fought with France over American territory in a war called the **French and Indian**

War, or the Seven Years' War. The war was expensive, and when it was over Britain needed to find a way to pay for it. Parliament decided to impose taxes on the colonists and use the tax money it collected to pay for its war **debts.** Parliament thought this was fair, since the war was fought to help colonists keep their land.

Rebellion

Many colonists **rebelled** when Parliament began to force them to pay these taxes. They believed that if they did not protest, Parliament would keep taxing them on more and more **goods.** The main reason they were angry was that they had no representation in Parliament. While the colonists had a voice in local government, colonists were not entitled to elect representatives to sail across the Atlantic Ocean and vote in Parliament. All of the members of Parliament lived in Great Britain and had little knowledge of everyday life in the colonies.

Part of the French and Indian War was fought in Canada. Below, British and French soldiers fight for control of Quebec, Canada.

Boycotts and Protests

One way **colonists** protested the taxes **Parliament** had imposed was by writing letters to newspapers, which then published them. Letter writers declared that by taxing them on everyday items such as molasses, playing cards, newspapers, and tea, Parliament was turning them into slaves. Another way colonists protested the taxes was by bothering tax collectors. Colonists shouted at them and sometimes even covered them in tar and feathers—a popular punishment in those days.

The Stamp Act Congress

Colonists did more than speak out against the taxes imposed on them by Parliament. In 1765, a group of **delegates** met in New York City at a gathering called the Stamp Act **Congress.** There, they wrote a statement to protest Parliament's Stamp Act, which put taxes on everyday items, especially those made from paper. The delegates agreed to **boycott** all British **goods,** figuring they would not have to pay taxes on items they did not buy.

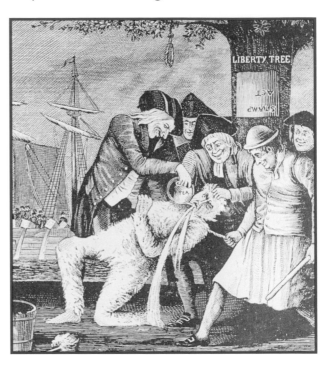

This man was tarred and feathered as punishment for being a tax collector.

Another way colonists protested the Stamp Act was to gather together in a public place and burn written versions of the Act.

Tea tax

Parliament **repealed** the Stamp Act in 1766. But to show that Parliament was still in charge, it quickly passed the Declaratory Act. This act stated that Parliament had the power to make any law it wished for the **colonies.** The next year, Parliament passed another act that forced the colonists to pay even more taxes. Eventually it repealed these taxes, except for a tax on tea.

The repeals did little to relieve the tensions in the colonies. Colonists felt that Parliament kept the tea tax as a way of showing that it had every right to control them. To make matters worse, Parliament sent British soldiers into Boston, Massachusetts, in response to a **rebellion** there against the taxes.

The Boston Tea Party

Things simmered in the colonies for a few years as the boycotts and taxes continued. Then, in December 1773, a group of colonists in Boston disguised as Mohawk Indians decided to protest the tea tax. They boarded three ships docked in Boston Harbor and tossed all the tea onboard into the harbor. This became known as the Boston Tea Party. When Parliament found out about the protest, it closed the port of Boston to all trade.

This cartoon from colonial times shows caged **loyalists** being fed by **patriots.** In the background is Boston Harbor, which the British closed in 1774.

The Colonies Band Together

When **Parliament** closed Boston's harbor and port, the **colonists** grew even more concerned. They realized that something would have to change—they could not continue to allow Parliament to impose such laws on them. On September 5, 1774, **delegates** from each colony met at the First Continental **Congress** in Philadelphia, Pennsylvania, to discuss their concerns. Delegates at the Congress agreed that they did not wish to declare independence from Britain. Instead, they started another **boycott** of British **goods** and agreed that if Parliament did not loosen its hold on Boston, they would meet again in May of 1775.

The Second Continental Congress

The Continental Congress did meet again in May of 1775. By that time, the situation in Massachusetts was heating up. A few days before the opening of Congress, members of the Massachusetts **militia** had fought with the British at the towns of Lexington and Concord. Most colonists were beginning to realize that if they wanted freedom, they would have to fight for it. Congress prepared by organizing the Continental Army. George Washington was selected to lead the army, and the **Revolutionary War** began.

The line of coffins at the top of this announcement represents colonists killed in the battles of Lexington and Concord, Massachusetts, in 1775.

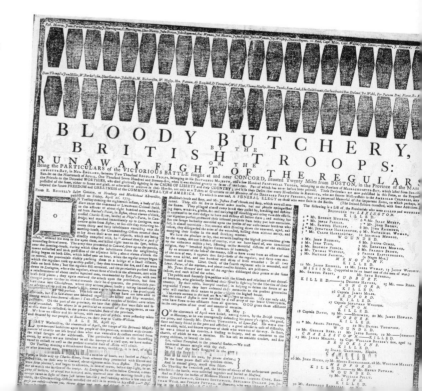

14

The Continental Congress continued its session into 1776. In the spring of that year, Massachusetts delegate John Adams recommended that each **colony** set up its own government, free from British control. Another delegate, Richard Henry Lee of Virginia, said that Congress should declare all the colonies to be independent from Britain.

The committee of five

Congress agreed with Lee's suggestion—on June 10 it selected a committee of five men to **draft** a formal document declaring independence. The five men were John Adams of Massachusetts, Benjamin Franklin of Pennsylvania, Thomas Jefferson of Virginia, Robert R. Livingston of New York, and Roger Sherman of Connecticut. The committee chose Jefferson, a well-educated man who had a talent for writing, to actually write the declaration. At 33, he was the committee's youngest member.

The Declaration of Independence was the most important document written in America up to that time. Its purpose was not only to declare independence— it was also a birth announcement. When Congress approved the document, a new country was born: The United States of America.

Richard Henry Lee's solution

On June 7, 1776, Congressman Richard Henry Lee of Virginia stood up to speak at the Second Continental Congress. He said:

[T]hese United Colonies are, and of a right ought to be, free and independent states, that they are absolved [set free] from all allegiance [loyalty] to the British Crown, and that all political connection between them and the state of Great Britain is, and ought to be, totally dissolved.

His motion was seconded by John Adams. On the next day, Congress began to discuss whether they should take the action that Lee and Adams suggested.

Drafting the Document

Thomas Jefferson wrote the Declaration of Independence in seventeen days. From time to time, he met with the senior members of the committee—John Adams and Benjamin Franklin—to discuss what to include or the kind of wording to use. But all of the committee members had an influence on the document, and each member holds an important place in U.S. history.

John Adams

John Adams may have contributed more to American independence than any other person. He was born in 1735 in Braintree, Massachusetts (now called Quincy in honor of his son, John Quincy Adams). Adams graduated from Harvard College in 1755. For a while he was a teacher and even thought of becoming a minister, but instead he became a lawyer. When **Parliament** passed the Stamp Act in 1765, Adams realized the need for independence from Britain. He was a Congressional **delegate** from 1774 to 1777. He sat on more than 90 committees, **chairing** 25 of them. Adams retired from **Congress** in 1777 and went back to his law practice. He was soon asked by Congress to be a **diplomat** in Europe—a job he held until 1788. In 1789, Adams became the first vice president of the United States, and from 1797 until 1801 he was president. He died on July 4, 1826, just a few hours after the death of another important U.S. figure, Thomas Jefferson.

The scraps of papers on the floor show that Franklin, Adams, and Jefferson wrote and discarded several versions of the Declaration.

Benjamin Franklin

Franklin had a long, interesting life. He was born in 1706 in Boston, Massachusetts. He had some schooling, but taught himself many things by reading and experimenting. When he was twelve, he went to work with his half brother who was a printer and newspaper publisher. Franklin submitted articles to the newspaper, though his name was kept a secret. He moved to Philadelphia, Pennsylvania, in 1723, and then went to London for two years. When he returned to Philadelphia, he resumed his printing career. He published *The Pennsylvania Gazette* and *Poor Richard's Almanac*. The latter was the second most popular publication in the **colonies**, after the Bible.

Franklin helped **found** libraries, schools, and hospitals. He was deputy postmaster for the colonies, as well as a **colonial agent** in England. For a long time, he was against the idea of American independence. However, as Parliament continued to tax the colonies, he began to change his mind. He even spoke in meetings of Parliament on behalf of the colonies. Franklin was the oldest delegate to sign the Declaration of Independence. He later went on to be a **commissioner** to France. In 1787, he became the head of a society to end slavery. Benjamin Franklin died in 1790.

COMMON SENSE;

ADDRESSED TO THE

INHABITANTS

OF

AMERICA,

On the following interesting

SUBJECTS.

I. Of the Origin and Design of Government in general, with concise Remarks on the English Constitution.

II. Of Monarchy and Hereditary Succession.

III. Thoughts on the present State of American Affairs.

IV. Of the present Ability of America, with some miscellaneous Reflections.

Man knows no Master save creating HEAVEN,
Or those whom choice and common good ordain.
THOMSON.

PHILADELPHIA;

Printed, and Sold, by R. BELL, in Third-Street.
MDCCLXXVI.

Thomas Paine's "common sense"

In January 1776, a **pamphlet** titled *Common Sense* was published in Philadelphia. The author of the pamphlet was Thomas Paine, who had come to the colonies from England only months earlier. In *Common Sense*, Thomas Paine wrote that people have rights to freedom and that the **colonists** would not be able to work out their problems with Great Britain. He encouraged the colonies to declare independence. His words did much to make colonists believe that they could, indeed, become a free nation with their own government.

The pamphlet sold quickly—about 150,000 copies in three months—and went on to be printed several more times. In all, nearly 500,000 copies were printed and sold!

IN CONGRESS.

The unanimous Declaration of the thirteen unite

This illustration shows the Committee of Five reviewing the Declaration of Independence. The globe at the bottom left corner depicts the new "America."

Thomas Jefferson

Jefferson was born in 1743 on his family's **plantation** in Virginia. As a child he had private **tutors.** In 1762, he graduated from the College of William and Mary in Williamsburg, Virginia. Jefferson went on to study law and became a lawyer in 1767. Besides being a lawyer and politician, he was also a planter, **architect,** writer, and scientist. He liked to change the design of everyday items to see if he could make them work better. Jefferson designed and built a home on his Virginia plantation named Monticello. In 1769, Jefferson was elected to the Virginia **legislature.** At the Continental **Congress,** he was known for his silence, but other **delegates** had read his writings and admired them. Jefferson was strongly anti-British from an early age. He became Virginia's governor after the **colony** became a free and independent state. Later he was a **diplomat** and the U.S. Minister to France. Jefferson was **secretary of state** under President George Washington and vice president under John Adams. He then went on to be president, serving two four-year **terms,** from

1801 to 1809. He retired to Monticello in 1809 and led an active life. In 1819, he **founded** the University of Virginia. On July 4, 1826, Thomas Jefferson died at the age of 83.

Robert R. Livingston

Livingston was born in New York City in 1746. He became a lawyer and was a delegate to the Continental Congress from 1775 to 1777. Livingston was a judge in the New York court system for 24 years. He swore George Washington into office as president in 1789. From 1781 to 1783, he was the U.S. secretary of foreign affairs. And from 1801 to 1804, he was the U.S. diplomat to France. Besides his work in politics and law, Livingston was interested in **agriculture**. He spent several years experimenting with different farming techniques. He died in 1813.

Roger Sherman

Sherman was born in 1721 in Massachusetts. He moved to Connecticut in 1743 and bought a store there. Sherman acted as county **surveyor** and held several town offices in New Milford, Connecticut. He had little schooling, but taught himself through reading. He became a lawyer in 1754. In 1755 he was elected to the colonial legislature. In 1761, he decided that he no longer wanted to be a lawyer. So, he moved to New Haven, Connecticut, and managed a store there. Sherman was also a county judge, then an associate judge of the Connecticut Superior Court. In 1784, he was elected mayor of New Haven, and in 1787, he was a delegate to the Constitutional Convention. Sherman later became a U.S. representative and then a **senator.** He died in 1793.

Jefferson Writes the Declaration

After Jefferson was given the job of writing the Declaration of Independence, he returned to the house where he was staying. The house was a three-story brick building at the corner of Market and Seventh Streets in Philadelphia. Jefferson had rented the entire second floor and wrote the Declaration in the **parlor** on that floor. He sat on a wooden chair that swiveled and used a portable writing desk that he designed. The desk had no legs—just a writing surface that could be placed onto a table or on someone's lap—and it slanted at different angles. The desk folded up into a carrying box so it could be easily moved. The desk had a drawer in which nibs, or writing points, for his pens were kept. Also in the drawer was sand, which Jefferson used to absorb any drops of ink that fell onto the paper.

This is the parlor where Jefferson wrote the Declaration. It is kept just the way it looked in 1776.

Thomas Jefferson, violinist

While Jefferson was writing the Declaration of Independence, he sometimes took a break and played his violin. Some historians believe that Jefferson was actually a very good violinist. They know he played some difficult pieces. While he was **courting** Martha Skelton, the woman who later became his wife, he played the violin for her. After they married they played duets, he on the violin and she on a small stringed instrument called a harpsichord.

Writing tools

Like most writers of his time, Jefferson used a pen called a quill to write the Declaration. A quill is a pen made from a feather, usually from a goose, duck, swan, or pheasant. The tip of the feather is cut to a point.

Jefferson wrote **drafts** of the Declaration on large sheets of paper. **Congressional** records and documents were often put into a kind of notebook. So, the left margin of the paper is wider than the right margin, allowing the pages to be bound into a book.

Jefferson kept the first draft of the Declaration all his life, and it still exists. In many places, words or entire lines are crossed out, and changes are written between the lines or in the margin.

With Jefferson was his personal servant, fourteen-year-old Bob Hemings. As Jefferson wrote hour after hour, Hemings made tea for him and brought him meals. The tea was probably bought illegally from Dutch **merchants,** and not English ones. Hemings also made sure there was plenty of oil in the lamp that provided light for the room.

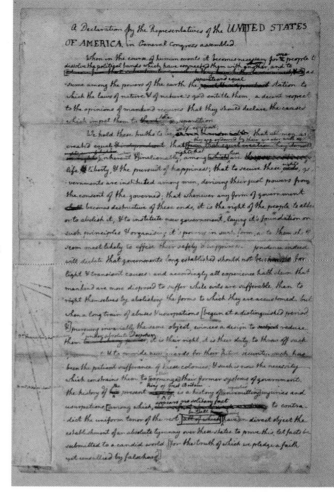

This page from Jefferson's first draft of the Declaration shows his changes.

Know It

As Jefferson wrote the Declaration, he tried to write what he believed the American public wanted to say. He said that the Declaration "was intended to be an expression of the American mind," and he wanted "to give to that expression the proper tone and spirit called for by the occasion."

Congress Revises the Declaration

Congress usually met in a large, open room. At times, with certain topics, **delegates** would talk amongst themselves.

During the seventeen days Jefferson worked on the Declaration of Independence, he took breaks to meet not only with John Adams and Benjamin Franklin, but also with the entire committee. After making the changes requested by committee members, Jefferson wrote a second **draft** of the document.

On June 28, 1776, the committee delivered its work to the rest of **Congress.** Members of Congress read the document, then decided that it was too long and removed quite a few words. At the time, Jefferson was unhappy about this, but most historians agree that the changes improved the Declaration. All together, about 80 changes were made to Jefferson's second draft, including the changes made by the committee.

Two sections were removed entirely. One section that was taken out referred to the people of Great Britain. The passage, the delegates thought, condemned the British people too harshly. Congress thought it would be better to show its **grievances** toward the king and **Parliament,** and not the British people.

The other passage Congress removed was about the slave trade. In the draft, Jefferson and the committee had condemned slavery as cruel and inhuman—even though some of them, including Jefferson himself, owned slaves. The passage was removed because it offended some members of Congress, especially Southern planters and wealthy **merchants** from New England who owned ships used in the slave trade.

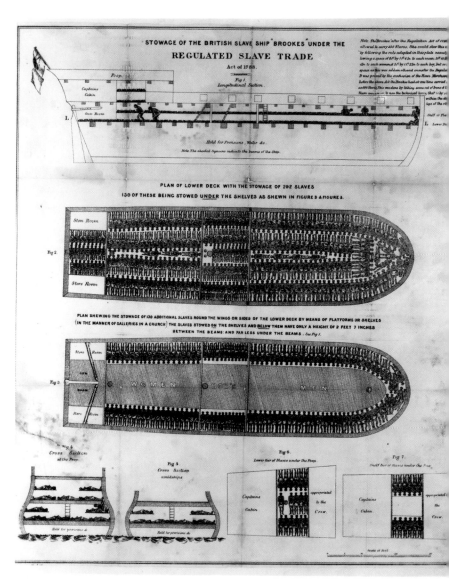

Slaves were packed tightly onto ships sailing to the **colonies.** In this cramped situation, slaves barely had room to move, or to breathe.

Know It

The majority of changes to the Declaration of Independence made by Congress had to do with writing style.

Independence

After the changes were made, **Congress** approved the Declaration of Independence on July 2, 1776. On July 4, the President of Congress, John Hancock of Massachusetts, signed the Declaration. Charles Thomson, secretary of Congress, also signed it. The public, however, still did not know about it, because Congress continued to work in secrecy. No one knows what happened to this first signed copy—it has been lost.

Printing the Declaration of Independence

After Congress approved the document, the committee of five was instructed to have it printed. John Dunlap, a Philadelphia printer, was given the job in the evening on July 4 —and it had to be ready the next morning! Dunlap, or the printer who set the type for the Declaration, made a few mistakes. Some punctuation was left out, for example, and other punctuation marks were put in that should not have been.

Dunlap printed the Declaration on a broadside—a large sheet of paper printed only on one side. While historians are not sure exactly how many copies were printed, most

John Hancock hoped to lead the Continental Army during the **Revolutionary War.** He was disappointed when Congress chose George Washington instead.

John Adams's prediction

Because the Declaration of Independence was approved on July 2, 1776, John Adams thought that Americans would celebrate that day for years to come. Adams had the celebration right, but July 4, the day the Declaration was signed, is the day Americans celebrate their independence, not July 2.

think it was around 500. Dunlap put his name at the bottom of the Declaration, which was a brave move. By adding his name, Dunlap showed not only the American people, but also the government of Britain, that he supported the ideas in the document. If the Revolutionary War failed, and the British continued to rule the **colonies,** those responsible for the **rebellion** would surely be hanged for **treason.** And Dunlap was adding his name to that list.

After the copies were made, they were rolled up and given to riders on horseback. The riders were to deliver copies to each colony. The news was out, and there was no turning back now.

Colonial printing

In colonial times, printing was a difficult task. Each letter and punctuation mark had to be set separately. The words were spelled out and placed backwards into a kind of box called a case. A printer had to read the words backwards to make sure he spelled them correctly. He also had to make sure to put even spaces between the words. After everything was set, the printer locked the case in a metal frame.

The case was then placed on a press. A printer rolled ink onto the letters, then put a sheet of paper in a form above the case. The paper was lowered onto the inked letters, then raised up again, leaving the type on the paper. After the paper was removed and dry, a printer washed it with a liquid called **alkali.**

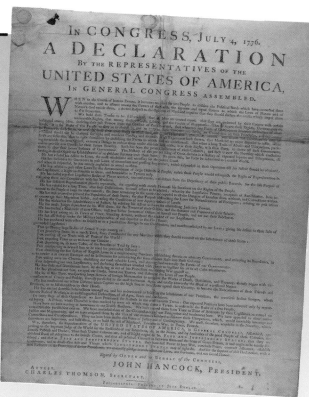

Early copies of the Declaration of Independence were printed with ink rolled onto raised letters.

25

Americans Hear the News

The copies of the Declaration of Independence printed by John Dunlap on the night of July 4, 1776, were sent to the **legislatures** of all thirteen new states. Copies also went to the councils of safety in the states, which were set up to oversee local **militias.** Commanding officers of the Continental Army also received copies and read them to their troops.

Because the copies were delivered by messengers on horseback, several weeks passed before everyone in the **colonies** could read the Declaration or listen as it was read aloud. On July 8, the Declaration of Independence was read publicly in some cities of Pennsylvania and New Jersey. In Philadelphia, crowds cheered after they heard the words of the document. The local militias fired their **muskets** into the air, and church

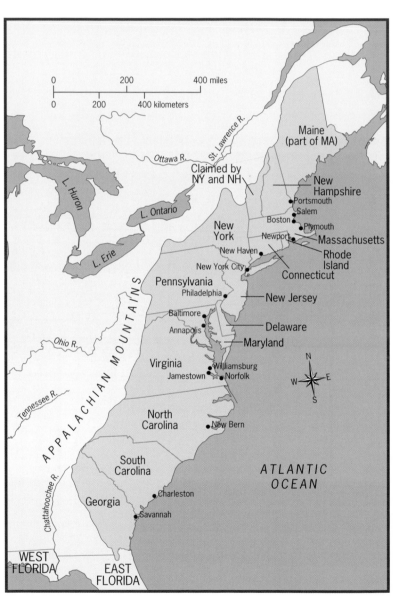

This map shows the original thirteen colonies at the time of the Declaration of Independence.

bells rang for hours. The next day the Declaration was read in New York City. Continental troops cheered, then ran to a statue of Britain's King George III and knocked it over.

On July 18, 1776, the Declaration was read in Boston, Massachusetts, where the presence of British troops was strong. Afterward, Bostonians destroyed statues of British kings and burned pictures of King George III. Newspapers also published the Declaration of Independence word for word. It first appeared in newspapers on July 9. It took a while for the copies to get to other states, especially in the South. The last city to hear the Declaration read aloud was Savannah, Georgia, where it was read at the end of August.

An amazing find

In 1989, a man in Pennsylvania bought an old painting at a flea market because he liked the frame. Once at home, he began to remove the painting from the frame. He noticed an old document behind the painting that he soon discovered was a copy of the Declaration of Independence! The copy seemed very old, but he figured it was only 50 or 100 years old and not worth any money.

Norman Lear

Later, he decided to have an expert look at the document. To his surprise, it was a Dunlap broadside—one of the original copies of the Declaration printed on the night of July 4, 1776, by John Dunlap. Only 25 copies of this broadside are known to exist today.

When he found out that the broadside was worth millions of dollars, the man decided to sell it at an **auction** in 1991. A buyer paid $2.4 million for the broadside. In 2000, the buyer resold it, and a television executive named Norman Lear bought it for $8.14 million dollars. Lear then organized a tour for the broadside called the Independence Road Trip.

The Introduction

The Declaration of Independence can be divided into five sections: the introduction, the **preamble,** the **indictment** of King George III, the **denunciation** of the British people, and the conclusion.

The introduction to the Declaration is a single paragraph made up of one long sentence. It reads:

> *When in the Course of human events, it becomes necessary for one people to dissolve* [cut] *the political bands which have connected them with another, and to assume among the powers of the earth, the separate and equal station* [place] *to which the Laws of Nature and of Nature's God entitle them, a decent respect to the opinions of mankind requires that they should declare the causes which impel* [lead] *them to the separation.*

The "political bands" are those that tie the **colonies** to Great Britain. In the introduction, Thomas Jefferson states that the time has come to cut those bands. Then he writes that the **colonists** believe it is time to be regarded as "separate and equal"—that is, they believe that their

Introduction ▶

Around the time of the Declaration of Independence, people started using the term "liberty" in reference to the colonies more often.

new nation should be independent and that they should rule it. Jefferson and **Congress** believed that the "Laws of Nature and of Nature's God" allowed them to act in such a manner. God, they believed, made everyone equal, and that gave colonists the right to seek liberty.

The introduction then goes on to say that the document will now declare the reasons why the colonists feel it necessary to be independent from Great Britain. Neither the United States nor Great Britain, however, are mentioned by name in the text.

At a Meeting of the TRUE Sons of Liberty, in the City of New-York, July 27, 1774, PROPERLY convened;

PRESENT,

JOHN CALVIN, JOHN KNOX, ROGER RUMPUS, &c. &c. &c.

1. RESOLVED, That in this general Time of resolving, we have as good a Right to resolve as the most resolute.

2. RESOLVED, That we have the whole Sense of the City, County, Province, and all the Colonies, concentrated in our own Persons.

3. RESOLVED, Therefore, that a general Congress (saving Appearances) would be unnecessary and useless.

4. RESOLVED, That the Distresses of our Brethren-in-the-Lord of Boston are unprecedented, illegal, and diabolical; the People of Massachusetts-Bay being thereby required to make Reparation for Damages and Trespasses by them done and committed, only in Support of their own proper and avowed Purposes to establish one GRAND REPUBLIC throughout this ill-governed CONTINENT; of which, and for the sole Good and Benefit of the whole, the MASSACHUSITES only propose themselves as the Heads and Directors; in order that the said Continent, for the future, may be more justly and equitably ruled, directed, and protected.

5. RESOLVED, Therefore, that WE will concur with them in every Measure for effectuating the above-said salutary Purpose; being convinced, as were their and our Forefathers, that this is the only Way whereby an effectual Stop may be put to the alarming Growth of PRELACY, QUAKERISM, and universal Liberty of Conscience; to all of which, by the most obliging Methods of prosecuting, persecuting, whipping, hanging, or drowning, both they and we have ever been sworn Enemies; and so will continue, (God willing) till the End of Time——be it ever so endless.

6. RESOLVED, That the fittest Persons to carry on this great, good, necessary and godly Work, are not such as the Freeholders, in their respective Counties and Colonies, have elected to be their Representatives they being supposed to be Men of Conscience and Understanding—but such only as OURSELVES; who have not been used to Speculation and Refinement; but simply fitted, by our Lives and Conversation, for right-forward Doings; which are the only Doings, in these distresful Times, that ought to go right forward.

7. RESOLVED, with our Brethren of this City, that these Resolves, and any we may afterwards see Reason to promulge, shall be approved by all sensible and good Men in our Parent Country; and that they will even make that ungracious Varlet LORD NORTH shake in his Shoes, (when he sees them) and ——in his Breeches.

8. RESOLVED, with our Brethren of South-Carolina, that we will pay the Expence of printing these Resolves.

9. RESOLVED, According to the third Resolve of our Brethren of New-Brunswick, that any Act or Acts of Parliament which prevent the Colonies from triumphing over the Liberties, sporting with the Lives, or at Will claiming the Properties of the Ministry, is a cruel Oppression in which all the Colonies are intimately concerned.

10. RESOLVED, with our Brethren of Annapolis, that the Non-Payment of Debts contracted with England, is the only Way to save the Credit of those, who have got no Money to pay their Debts with.

11. RESOLVED, That a strict Adherence to a Non-Importation and Non-Exportation Agreement, which was so easily effected, and so faithfully observed, in the Time of the Stamp-Act, is the only certain Means of coming at the naked Truth; without which we shall never be able to unveil the covert, and close, and cloked Designs of the d——d Ministry, to ruin us.

12. RESOLVED, That because Boston is undeservedly chastised, all the other Colonies ought to be chastised deservedly.

13. RESOLVED, That it is a General Mark of Patriotism, to eat the King's Bread, and abuse him for giving it.

14. RESOLVED, That the best Way of approving our Loyalty, is to spit in the said King's Face; as that may be the Means of opening his Eyes.

15. RESOLVED, lastly, That every Man, Woman, or Child, who doth not agree with our Sentiments, whether he, she, or they, understand them or not, is an Enemy to his Country, wheresoever he was born, and a Jacobite in Principle, whatever he may think of it; and that he ought at least to be tarred and feathered, if not hanged, drawn and quartered; all Statutes, Laws and Ordinances whatsoever to the contrary notwithstanding.

By Order of the MEETING,

EBENEZER SNUFFLE, SECRETARY.

IN CONGRESS. JULY 4.

The unanimous Declaration of the thirteen united States of

The Preamble

The section of the Declaration after the introduction is called the **preamble**. The preamble also does not mention Great Britain or the United States by name, nor does it mention any specific details that drove **colonists** to seek independence. It states:

We hold these truths to be self-evident [visible], *that all men are created equal, that they are endowed by their Creator with certain unalienable* [incapable of being transferred] *Rights, that among these are Life, Liberty, and the pursuit of Happiness. That to secure these rights, Governments are instituted among Men, deriving their just powers from the consent of the governed. That whenever any Form of Government becomes destructive of these ends, it is the Right of the People to alter or to* **abolish** *it, and to institute* [create] *new Government, laying its foundation on such principles and organizing its powers in such form, as to them shall seem most likely to effect their Safety and Happiness. Prudence* [caution], *indeed, will dictate that Governments long established should not be changed for light and transient* [temporary] *causes; and accordingly all experience hath shewn that mankind are more disposed to suffer, while evils are sufferable, than to right themselves by abolishing the forms to which they are accustomed. But when a long train of* **abuses** *and* **usurpations,** *pursuing invariably the same Object evinces* [reveals] *a design to reduce them under absolute Despotism* [government in which ruler has unlimited power], *it is their right, it is their duty, to throw off such Government, and to provide new Guards for their future security.*

Preamble ▶

In this section, Jefferson brings up the rights that belong to all people from birth. Included in those rights is life, meaning that people should not have to live in fear for their lives. The government would set up laws and systems, such as the court system, that would protect their lives and punish those who

Early flags had thirteen stars and thirteen stripes to represent the original thirteen American colonies.

murdered others. Liberty is another right—the right to be free. The third right listed is the pursuit of happiness. This means that each person should be able to do what makes him or her happy. In those days, this especially meant that people should be able to worship and practice their religion without **interference** from the government.

The Declaration states that to make sure people had those rights, people set up governments. The governments are made up of the people. People have the right to change the government if it is not protecting their rights. Here is where the Declaration begins to focus on the reason the colonists wished to form their own government. The British government, the writers felt, was not protecting their rights. Instead, it was taking some of those rights away.

Jefferson then goes on to write that governments should not be ended for "light and transient causes." This means that the reasons for getting rid of a government should be serious ones. But, he continues, when many abuses have been inflicted upon the people—referring to the abuses **Parliament** was inflicting upon the **colonies**—it is not only the right, but the duty of the people to get rid of that government and establish a new one.

The List of Grievances

After the introduction and the **preamble,** the Declaration goes into more detail about why the American **colonies** feel the need to declare their independence. This section is called the list of **grievances.** It starts by saying that the colonies have patiently suffered as their rights have been violated. Now it is time to change the way the colonies are governed. The next sentence states that "The history of the present King of Great Britain is a history of repeated injuries and **usurpations,** all having in direct object the establishment of an absolute **Tyranny** over these states." The word "usurpations" and the phrase after it mean that the king is acting in ways that are beyond his power. In doing so, he is taking away the rights of the people. The goal of the king, the document says, is to establish tyranny, which is when one ruler has absolute power.

27 charges

Then the Declaration goes on to list the things the king has done to prove that he is trying to establish a tyranny. This is the longest section of the Declaration. It lists a total of 27 charges. The first group of charges include ways in which the king alone has **abused** his power. For example, one charge says of the king that "He has dissolved Representative Houses repeatedly, for opposing with manly firmness his invasions on the rights of the people."

This cartoon was published August 1, 1779. It shows America as a horse, throwing its master—Great Britain—off its back. This action represents the separation of the colonies and Great Britain as proposed in the Declaration of Independence.

One colony this occurred in was Virginia. The colony's **legislature,** called the House of Burgesses, was closed by the royal governor, who was acting on behalf of the king. Another charge says that "He has kept among us, in times of peace, Standing Armies without the Consent of our Legislature." This refers to the British troops that were stationed in Boston and other colonial cities without approval from the **colonists.**

The second group lists charges that show how the king joined with **Parliament** in imposing **unjust** laws on colonists. These laws include, as listed in the Declaration, "cutting off our Trade with all parts of the world" and "imposing taxes on us without our consent." Many other **injustices** are listed as well.

The third group of charges discusses how the king has declared war on the colonies and lists the things he has done. This list accuses the king of many abuses, including sending soldiers hired from other countries to fight in the colonies. This example refers to the Hessian, or German, soldiers who were paid to fight alongside the British during the **Revolutionary War.**

Hessian soldiers were often sold by their leader to fight on the side of the British.

The Denunciation of the British People

After the introduction, the **preamble**, and the list of **grievances**, is what is referred to by many historians as the **denunciation** of the British people. The passage states:

*Nor have We been wanting in attention to our Brittish brethren [brothers]. We have warned them from time to time of attempts by their **legislature** to extend an unwarrantable jurisdiction [authority] over us. We have reminded them of the circumstances of our **emigration** and settlement here. We have appealed to their native justice and magnanimity [spirit], and we have conjured [asked] them by the ties of our common kindred [relatives] to disavow [deny] these **usurpations**, which, would inevitably [soon] interrupt our connections and correspondence. They too have been deaf to the voice of justice and of consanguinity [blood]. We must, therefore, acquiesce [accept] in the necessity, which denounces our Separation, and hold them, as we hold the rest of mankind, Enemies in War, in Peace Friends.*

This copy of the Declaration of Independence was engraved, designed, and printed by John Binn in 1818.

The Revolutionary War lasted from 1775 to 1783. Colonists and British soldiers fought fierce battles for control of the **colonies.**

"Our Brittish brethren"

The "Brittish brethren" referred to here are the British people. All of the signers of the Declaration of Independence had British ancestors. Some signers were even born in England! Because of this, **colonists** were tied closely to the British, not just by politics but by blood. In this passage, Jefferson reminds the British people that many colonists have written to them or spoken to them about the **abuse** of the king's and **Parliament's** power. Most colonists believed the British to be fair and just people. But this passage reminds them that they have stood by and done nothing while colonists have suffered. Jefferson felt that the British people would not listen to what he and **Congress** considered to be reasonable complaints by colonists.

The last sentence in this passage states that because the British have not stood up for the rights of the colonists, they will now be considered enemies. But this condition would only last as long as the **Revolutionary War** lasted. When the war ended, colonists would once again consider the British friends.

The Conclusion

The final part of the Declaration of Independence is the conclusion. The conclusion states:

*We, therefore, the Representatives of the united States of America, in General **Congress**, Assembled, appealing to the Supreme Judge of the world for the rectitude [righteousness] of our intentions, do, in the Name, and by Authority of the good People of these **Colonies**, solemnly publish and declare, That these United Colonies are, and of Right ought to be Free and Independent States; that they are Absolved [set free] from all Allegiance [obligation] to the British Crown, and that all political connection between them and the State of Great Britain, is and ought to be totally dissolved [cut]; and that as Free and Independent States, they have full Power to levy [wage] War, conclude Peace, contract Alliances, establish Commerce, and to do all other Acts and Things which Independent States may of right do. And for the support of this Declaration, with a firm reliance [confidence] on the Protection of divine Providence, we mutually pledge to each other our Lives, our Fortunes and our sacred Honor.*

Conclusion ▶

The United States

It is here that the new country is first and formally called "The United States of America." The conclusion makes it clear that the United States is no longer tied to the British crown, or the king. Further, it states that now that the country has declared its independence, it is free to carry on a war with Great Britain. It is also free to have the other **privileges** that independent nations have. In this passage, Jefferson refers to God or to a greater being twice when he writes "the Supreme Judge of the world" and "Divine Providence." The **patriots** who signed the document believed that their quest for independence was right not only in their eyes, but in the eyes of a higher power as well.

Revolution

The last sentence of this passage speaks to the seriousness of what Congress was doing. War was already going on in the colonies between the British and the **colonists.** With the Declaration of Independence, the country was starting a **revolution.** Americans now had to fight the British until either one side or the other surrendered. If the Americans were forced to surrender, the British government could arrest those responsible for the revolution and hang them. The **delegates** who put their names on this important document truly were pledging their lives to the cause of freedom.

When Americans heard the Declaration of Independence read aloud for the first time, many cheered and some pulled down statues of Britain's King George III.

Engrossing the Declaration

On July 19, 1776, **Congress** had the Declaration of Independence **engrossed** on parchment paper. This meant that a professional **calligrapher** sat down and carefully copied the document. While there is no record of who did this job, historians believe it was probably Timothy Matlack, who was an assistant to Charles Thomson.

People in **colonial** times used paper made from wood pulp, as we do today. However, special documents were written on parchment because it was a strong material that lasted longer than paper. Parchment is an ancient kind of writing material that was first used more than 1,000 years ago. It is made from animal skin, usually the skin of a sheep, calf, or goat. All fur or hair is stripped or scraped from the skin. Then the skin is stretched on a frame and scraped some more. As it dries, it becomes strong, like a thin piece of leather.

This painting shows Timothy Matlack in about 1790. He was a Pennsylvania **delegate** to the Continental Congress from 1780–87. Matlack lived to be more than 99 years old!

The writer engrossed the Declaration using a fancy, flowing style of lettering called calligraphy. To write, a calligrapher used a quill, which is a feather from a goose, duck, swan, or pheasant. The tip of the feather was cut to a point. The ink used to engross the Declaration was made from iron gall. This ink is made from oak trees and several kinds of dyes.

Travels of the Declaration

After it was **engrossed,** the Declaration of Independence was given to Charles Thomson for safekeeping. He kept the document in the Philadelphia State House, where **Congress** met, until 1783. He then moved it as Congress met in various other cities.

When George Washington became president in 1790, the Declaration of Independence was given to the **secretary of state.** The first secretary of state was the writer of the document, Thomas Jefferson. He kept the document in City Hall on Wall Street in New York City—where Congress was meeting at the time. Later in 1790, the seat of the U.S. government moved back to Philadelphia, Pennsylvania, so the Declaration was moved there, too.

Washington, D.C.

In 1800, the new **federal** city of Washington, D.C., became the permanent home of the government. The Declaration of Independence was kept at the War Office building from 1800 until 1814, when it was moved to a safe place. The British were back in the United States fighting the War of 1812. As the British approached Washington, D.C., the Declaration, along with the U.S. **Constitution,** was packed in a linen sack by then Secretary of State James Monroe. The documents were first stored in a barn

Know It

The War of 1812
The War of 1812 was fought in North America between 1812 and 1814. It again found Americans fighting the British for their independence.

in Virginia, then at the home of the Littlejohn family in Leesburg, Virginia. Monroe's move was a wise one, because when the British entered Washington, D.C., they set fire to many buildings, including the White House. The documents were returned to Washington, D.C., after the war ended in 1814. In 1820, the documents were put into the new Department of State building.

In 1841, the secretary of state decided to display the Declaration of Independence on the wall in the Patent Office Building. It was framed and hung on the wall for many years. Its location was, unfortunately, across from a window, and the sunlight that hit the document caused the ink to fade. By the nation's 100th birthday in 1876, the Declaration looked old and worn. Still, it hung on the wall until 1894, when it was locked in a safe.

Fort Knox

In the 1920s, **conservators** examined the document and decided it should be sealed between two plates of glass and kept away from light. In 1924, the Declaration was moved to the Library of Congress, where it remained —except during World War II—until 1944. In 1941 during the war, the U.S. naval base at Pearl Harbor, Hawaii, was attacked. Government officials feared more attacks could come. To save important U.S. documents, they packed them into bronze containers and moved them to Fort Knox, Kentucky. They were returned to the Library of Congress in 1944, but were moved to the NARA in 1952.

On December 13, 1952, the Declaration of Independence was placed in a permanent display case at the NARA in Washington, D.C.

The Declaration on Display

Today, the Declaration of Independence is kept with the other **Charters of Freedom**—the U.S. **Constitution** and the **Bill of Rights**—at the headquarters of the NARA in Washington, D.C. The documents are on display in the **rotunda** of the building, and the display is open to the public.

Keeping the Declaration safe

From 1952 to 1998, the Declaration of Independence was stored in a case made from two sheets of glass edged with copper. The document was laid against handmade paper and a glass spacer was inserted to make sure the glass did not rub the parchment. Oxygen was removed from the case and another gas, helium, was inserted. Helium was used because it does not damage documents the way oxygen does. Then the two sheets of glass were sealed with a lead ribbon. The bulletproof glass the document was stored behind had special filters so light would not damage it.

In 1987, a three million dollar camera and a computer—that together make up the Charters Monitoring System—were purchased to check the Charters of Freedom regularly and make sure they remain in good condition. The system looks for flaking and fading ink, and it can tell

The exhibit cases that were "state of the art" in 1952, were out-of-date by the time the exhibit closed in 1998.

See the Declaration of Independence

You can see the Declaration of Independence at the National Archives building in Washington, D.C. The rotunda where the Declaration is exhibited is on Constitution Avenue. Be prepared to wait in line if you go—more than 5,000 people visit the exhibit each day!

You can also view the Declaration of Independence online at http://www.archives.gov/exhibit_hall/charters_of_freedom/images/us_declaration_preview.jpg.

if ink is rubbing onto the glass in front of the document. It takes one-inch (2.5-centimeter) photographs of the document from time to time, then checks each photograph to see whether anything has changed.

At night, after the exhibit closes, a special machine lowers the Charters of Freedom into a vault that lies 22 feet (6.7 meters) below the exhibit hall. The vault weighs 55 tons (50 metric tons) and is made of steel and concrete. The vault is used to further protect the documents when the NARA is closed.

Improving the display

In 1998, the public exhibit at the National Archives closed so **conservators** could **restore** the documents. The Declaration of Independence was carefully removed from its case and closely checked for any damage. The document was restored and put into a new case that was made based on the most recent scientific findings. The case is made from a strong substance called titanium, and is filled with a gas called argon to protect the writing.

The Charters of Freedom remain behind bulletproof glass, and they are still lowered into a vault at the end of each day. The restored Charters of Freedom are now back on display in their new cases. The remodeled NARA rotunda reopened in September 2003. The remodeling was done to better display the documents to the public.

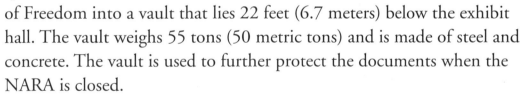

Working with the Declaration

Mary Lynn Ritzenthaler carefully cleans a document so that people can read it more easily.

According to Mary Lynn Ritzenthaler, who is the Chief of the Document Conservation Laboratory at the NARA, the Declaration of Independence is in fair condition today. Because it was exposed to light for so long while hanging in the U.S. Patent Office, the ink is faded in some spots. In particular, the signatures are faded, because different types of ink were used when different people signed. Also, the document was kept rolled up for many years, and ink smudged as it made contact with the rolled parchment.

Restoring the Declaration

Along with another **conservator,** Kitty Nicholson, Ms. Ritzenthaler worked on **restoring** the document when it was removed. She was honored to be one of the few people allowed to handle the document. In fact, she counts it as the most exciting experience she has had since joining the National Archives. Along with the other **Charters** of Freedom, Ms. Ritzenthaler and Ms. Nicholson examined the Declaration, wrote a report on its condition, and did some conservation work on it.

Conservators must be aware of what can harm an old document. This conservator wears gloves before handling a document from 1803.

Becoming an archivist

Mary Lynn Ritzenthaler encourages young people who are interested in history and science to consider becoming **archivists** or document conservators. Those who do this kind of work have to be good at working with their hands, because they do detailed work on old documents that must be carefully handled. Some knowledge of science is important, since archivists and conservators must be aware of how different chemicals interact in various environments. Besides working with papers and books, Ms. Ritzenthaler explained that people who do this kind of work could also work with photographs, **textiles,** furniture, and other **artifacts.**

The importance of the Declaration of Independence

The Declaration of Independence is as important to Americans today as it was in 1776. It reminds us of how and why our forefathers fought for freedom. It also reminds us of the principles on which our freedom is based. As Ms. Ritzenthaler said, "Such documents tell the story of our nation . . . how decisions were made and how compromises were reached. They also reflect the ideals and optimism [positive feelings] of the founding citizens . . . they also document the various participants, the roles they played, the arguments and debates they engaged in, and the alliances that were forged."

Glossary

abolish put an end to

abuse improper or unfair treatment

agriculture study of various kinds of farming

alkali kind of salt that comes from the ashes of plants

architect person who designs buildings

archivist person who works to restore and preserve public records and historical papers

artifact object made and used by someone in the past

auction public sale in which things are sold to those who offer to pay the most

Bill of Rights document that lists the rights and privileges of all people in a nation

boycott refusal to do business with or engage in other activities with a person, business, organization, or government; usually done to focus attention on a disagreement with that party

calligrapher person who writes out important documents for a living using a large, fancy kind of handwriting

chair lead a meeting or discussion

charter official document granting, guaranteeing, or showing the limits of the rights and duties of the group to which it is given

colonial agent someone sent to another country to work out business affairs for persons who live in the colony

colonist person who lives in a colony

colony settlement in a new territory that is tied to an established nation

commissioner representative of a government sent to take care of matters in another country

Congress formal meeting of delegates for discussion and usually action on some question; lawmaking body of the U.S. government

conservator person who is responsible for the care, restoration, and repair of documents and other historical artifacts

constitution document that outlines the basic principles of a government

council elected group of people set up to give advice or pass laws

court seek the liking of

debt amount of money owed

delegate person sent as a representative to a meeting or conference

denunciation expression of strong dislike for something or the way something has been done

deteriorate become damaged in quality, condition, or value

diplomat person sent by one government to negotiate with another

draft prepare; unfinished form of a piece of writing

emigration leaving one region or country to live in another

engross prepare the final handwritten or printed text of an official document

federal one central government that oversees smaller units; the smaller units, such as states, also have their own governments

found start something, like a school

French and Indian War war fought between Great Britain and France in the American colonies from 1754 to 1763. Some Native Americans fought with the French, while others fought with the British.

good thing that can be bought or sold

grievance cause of uneasiness or annoyance; formal complaint

humidity amount of moisture, or water, in the air

indictment statement that shows strong disapproval

injustice unfair action

interfere become involved in the affairs of others

legislature group of elected individuals who make laws for those who elect them

loyalist person who remains loyal to a particular cause; during the American Revolution, a loyalist was someone who remained loyal to Great Britain

merchant store owner or trader

militia ordinary citizens with some military training banded together in a military unit

musket kind of gun used during the Revolutionary War

pamphlet booklet with no cover, usually made of paper folded into smaller parts

Parliament group of elected officials that forms the main ruling body of Great Britain

parlor room of a house used to entertain guests

patriot person who supports his or her country; during the American Revolution, those who fought for freedom from Great Britain

plantation large farm, usually in the South, often with slaves

preamble introductory statement

primary source original copy of a journal, letter, newspaper, document, or image

privilege benefit or favor

Puritan member of a religious group that settled in New England in the sixteenth and seventeenth centuries; Puritans rejected the services of the Church of England as too formal

Quaker member of a religious group called Quakerism that began in the mid-seventeenth century; some Quakers traveled to North America on the *Mayflower* to practice their religion freely

quest journey in which something is sought

rebellion open fight against one's government; open opposition to authority

reconciliation settle, as in a dispute

repeal overrule or dismiss; in Congress, to say "no" to an idea, proposal, or amendment

restore put or bring back to an earlier or original state

revolution overthrow one government and replace with a new government created by those originally governed

Revolutionary War American fight for independence from British rule between 1775–1783

rotunda round building covered by a dome; or large round room

secondary source written account of an event by someone who studied a primary source or sources

secretary of state person in the U.S. government who is responsible for foreign affairs

senator member of the legislative branch in a government

stack structure of bookshelves for storing books, often used in libraries

statesman person who is active in government and who gives good advice in making policies

subject person under the authority or control of another; person who owes loyalty to a monarch or state

surveyor person who measures land to determine boundaries and geographical features

term period of time fixed by law

textile item made from woven cloth

treason crime of trying to overthrow the government of one's country

tutor private teacher; tutors often teach one student, or a small group of students

tyranny government in which one ruler has all the power

unjust unfair

usurpation take and hold unfairly by force

More Books to Read

Burgan, Michael. *The Declaration of Independence.* Mankato, Minn.: Compass Point Books, 2000.

Smolinski, Diane. *Important People of the Revolutionary War.* Chicago: Heinemann Library, 2002.

Stein, R. Conrad. *The National Archives.* Danbury, Conn.: Franklin Watts, Inc., 2002.

Index